WHAT DOES MONEY LOOK LIKE IN DIFFERENT PARTS OF THE WORLD?

MONEY LEARNING FOR KIDS

Children's Growing Up & Facts of Life Books

BABY PROFESSOR
EDUCATION KIDS

Speedy Publishing LLC
40 E. Main St. #1156
Newark, DE 19711
www.speedypublishing.com

Different countries around the world use different kinds of money. Several countries maintain their own. The government backs the money and it is known as "legal tender", which is money that has to be accepted as payment in that particular country. In this book, you will learn about some of the different forms of currencies throughout the world.

Retro filtered picture of banknotes from all over the world.

While there are many different forms of money, there are a few currencies that are used or accepted in many different countries and regions. Some of these are listed below:

THE EURO

This is the official currency of what is known as the Eurozone. The Eurozone is comprised of 19 out of the 28 states that are members of the European Union. These are: **Spain, Slovenia, Slovakia, Portugal, the Netherlands, Malta, Luxembourg, Lithuania, Latvia, Italy, Ireland, Greece, Germany, France, Finland, Estonia, Cyprus, Belgium** and **Austria.**

It is also used officially by four additional European countries and the institutions of the European Union, and by two others unilaterally. Consequently, it is used by some 337 million Europeans daily as of 2015. It is also used by several overseas territories of EU members.

Euro money banknotes.

Euro was officially named on December 16, 1995 in Madrid. It was introduced to the world financial markets on January 1, 1999, for an accounting currency, to replace the prior *ECU (European Currency Unit)* at the ratio of 1:1 (US $1.1743). On January 1, 2002, the physical euro coin and banknote entered circulation. Once in circulation it became the day-to-day currency of the original members and by May of 2002 it had totally replaced the previous currencies.

Several hundred euro banknotes stacked by value.

While its value subsequently dropped to $0.8252 U.S. Dollars towards the end of 2002, it peaked at $1.038 U.S. Dollars on July 18, 2008. Starting late in 2009, the Euro became immersed in a European sovereign-debt crisis leading to the conception of the European Financial Stability Facility and other reforms to stabilize concerns regarding Greek debt and the troubled banking sector of Spain.

Japanese Yen.

THE JAPANESE YEN

The Japanese Yen is known as Japan's official currency. Following the U.S. dollar and the euro, the yen is the third greatest traded currency. It also is widely used for reserve currency, following the U.S. dollar, euro, and the pound sterling.

The yen concept was an element of the government of Meiji program to modernize Japan's economy. Prior to the Meiji Restoration, Japan's feudal fiefs distributed their own money leading to the pursuit of a currency that would be uniform throughout all the country. The New Currency Act of 1871 got rid of this and created the yen, defined as 1.5 g of gold or 24.26 g of silver.

Japanese currency notes.

The yen started losing its value after World War II. In order to steady the economy of Japan, the yen exchange rate became fixed at ¥360 per $1 as part of the *Bretton Woods system.* In 1971, when that system ended, it became devalued and they decided to allow it to float.

In 1973, it rose to a high of ¥271 per $1, and then went through periods of appreciation and depreciation because of the oil crisis in 1973, coming to a worth of ¥227 per $1 by 1980.

Japanese Yen.

The government of Japan has continued to maintain this policy of intervening with the currency since 1973, and is considered to be following a *"Dirty Float"* regime. This continues until present day.

Japanese Yen

THE BRETTON WOODS SYSTEM

Bretton Woods is a system of managing money which established policies for financial and commercial relations among Japan, Australia, Western Europe, Canada, and the United States during the middle of the 20th century.

570740

The Royal B of Scotland

PROMISE TO PAY THE BEARER ON

FIVE POUND

STERLING

AT THEIR HEAD OFFICE HERE IN EDINBURG

BY ORDER OF THE BOARD
20th JANUARY 2005

*Banknote for five pounds sterling
produced by the Royal Bank of Scotland.*

THE BRITISH POUND STERLING

More well known as the pound, the British Pound Sterling is the official currency of Tristan da Cunha, the British Antarctic Territory, South Georgia and South Sandwich Islands, the Isle of Man, Guernsey, Jersey, and the United Kingdom. It is divided into 100 pence.

There are several other nations that do not use the sterling, however, they use currencies also named the pound. At different times, it was known as commodity money, or bank notes, and was backed by gold and silver.

Currently, it is considered fiat money, which is backed by the economy wherever it is accepted. This currency is the oldest currency of the world that continues to be in use, and has been continued to be used since its beginning.

It is the fourth most-traded currency of the foreign exchange market, following the U.S. dollar, the euro, and the Japanese yen.

Pound sterling.

RATES OF EXCHANGE

As you travel to a different country, you will want to obtain local money by exchanging your money for that of the other country. This process is done by using the exchange rates. One example would be if you were to travel to Europe and you wanted to trade your U.S. Dollars for 100 Euros. If the current rate of exchange was 1 Euro for 1.3 Dollars, it would cost you 130 Dollars for 100 Euros.

Dollar, euro coin on euro background.

To find the most recent exchange rates for various countries, you can check on the internet. Exchange rates may vary and various institutions or banks may charge a fee for making these exchanges.

THE GOLD STANDARD

Is money worth anything? In the past, countries held gold to represent the money that had been printed. Each bill or coin would be backed by the gold that was held in a giant vault. This is no longer done. Typically, they do have what is known as the *"Gold Reserves"* to help back it, but it's the government and the economy that back its value.

Close-up of a 20 dollar banknote note and gold bullions.

Canadian banknotes.

POLYMER BANKNOTES

Most banknotes are made from a certain type of cotton paper. However, there are banknotes that consist of a polymer, *Biaxially Oriented Polypropylene (BOPP)*, known as Polymer Banknotes. These notes are able to contain several security features which are not included in the paper banknotes, such as using metameric links.

These notes last quite a bit longer than the paper versions, resulting in decrease of the impact to the environment as well as reduced replacement and production costs.

The Reserve Bank of Australia, Commonwealth Scientific and Industrial Research Organization and The University of Melbourne developed the first modern polymer banknotes. In 1988, the first polymer banknotes were introduced in Australia and in 1996, they completely switched to this type of banknote.

Australian currency banknotes all denominations.

Countries that have followed and totally switched are Vietnam, Kuwait, Romania, Papua New Guinea, New Zealand, Canada and Brunei.

Nepal, Republic of Maldives, Trinidad and Tobago, Nicaragua, The Gambia, Chili, Cape Verde, and the United Kingdom have started introducing these banknotes into circulation.

Dollar notes in New Zealand currency..

Zimbabwe currency.

LOCAL CURRENCIES

In the fascinating world of economics, a local currency is considered to be currency which is not backed by a national government, and is intended for use only in a very small area. Some advocates argue that this will enable a region that is depressed economically to regain strength by allowing the people living in that region a way of exchange in which they can exchange services and goods produced locally.

This concept's opponents argue that the local currency will create a barrier that interferes with the economies of scale and comparative advantage, and may also create a method for tax evasion.

This type of currency also can come alive when there is an economic turmoil that involves their national currency. The Argentinian economic crisis of 2002 is an example, where IOU's that were issued by the local government soon took on many of the local currency characteristics.

A selection of Zimbabwe Reserve Bank bearer cheques printed between July 2007 to July 2008 to illustrate the hyperinflation rate in Zimbabwe.

The original LETS currency, founded in the early 1980s on Vancouver Island is a perfect example. The Canadian Central Bank's rates for lending went up to 14% in 1982, which then raised the chartered bank rates up to a high of 19%. The currency and credit scarcity that resulted left the island citizens with very few options other than to create their own local currency.

LIST OF WORLD CURRENCIES

Here is a list of some of the currencies used throughout the world. While countries other than the United States have a currency known as the Dollar, the rates of exchange vary.

- Australia - Dollar

- Brazil - Real

- Canada - Dollar

- Chile - Peso

- China - Yuan or Renminbi

- Czech Republic - Koruna

- Denmark - Krone
- France - Euro
- Germany - Euro
- Greece - Euro
- Hong Kong - Dollar
- Hungary – Forint
- India – Rupee
- Indonesia - Rupiah
- Israel - New Shekel
- Italy - Euro
- Japan – Yen
- Malaysia - Ringgit
- Mexico - Peso
- Netherlands - Euro
- New Zealand - Dollar
- Norway - Krone
- Pakistan - Rupee
- Philippines - Peso

American dollars, European euro, Swiss franc, Chinese yuan and Russian Ruble bills.

- Poland - Zloty

- Russia - Ruble

- Saudi Arabia - Riyal

- Singapore - Dollar

- South Africa - Rand

- South Korea - Won

- Spain - Euro

- Sweden - Krona

- Switzerland - Franc

- Taiwan - Dollar

- Turkey - Lira

- United Kingdom - Pound Sterling

- United States - Dollar

Turkish Banknotes.

DID YOU KNOW?

Queen Elizabeth II's portrait has been on money in 33 various countries.

In 44 B.C., Julius Caesar was the first live person featured on a coin.

Folded twenty dollar bills in New Zealand currency.

Some stores in different countries accept different forms of currency. One example would be in Denmark's tourist section where they might accept both their form of currency known as the Danish krone, as well as the euro.

For additional information on foreign currency you can visit your local library, research the internet and ask questions of your teachers, family and friends.

MAJOR WORLD CURRENCIES